What Men Want

What Men Secretly Want, What Men Really Want In a Woman and How to Make Men Chase You

Amelia Farris

www.southshorepublications.com

Copyright © 2015 SouthShore Publications

All rights reserved.

Although the author and publisher have made every effort to ensure that the information in this book was correct at press time, the author and publisher do not assume and hereby disclaim any liability to any party for any loss, damage, or disruption caused by errors or omissions, whether such errors or omissions result from negligence, accident, or any other cause.

ISBN-13: 978-1516994168

ISBN-10: 1516994167

CONTENTS

Introduction 1

How Much Do Looks Matter? 4

    Men Are Visual 4

    Does Weight Matter? 5

    Personal Hygiene 7

Personality 10

    Nagging 10

    Sensitivity 11

    Conflict Resolution 12

    Invite Him In 13

    Compromise 14

    Let Him Help You 16

Stand Out From The Crowd 19

    Thank Him 19

    Positive Energy 21

Mind Games 23

    Playing it Cool 23

    Limiting Your Time Together 25

The Importance of Sex 28

Sex and Dating 28

Having Great Sex to Keep a Man Coming Back 30

Sexual Energy 31

The Importance of Kissing 32

Compliment Their Body 32

Slow Things Down 33

Be Vocal 34

Conclusion 36
Final Thoughts 39

INTRODUCTION

Do you want to learn the secrets about what men really want from a woman? Do you want men to simply be crazy about you and have eyes for no other woman? Well in this short book you will find out the surprising truth about how to attract and keep pretty much any guy you want.

Maybe you have had a string of failed relationships for whatever reason and you're feeling disheartened by your experiences with dating and relationships so far. Don't worry, we all feel like this from time to time and there are ways to help ensure this cycle stops today.

You don't have to be a supermodel to do this. Looks are just one piece of the jigsaw. You don't have to be young, women of any age can use this advice. Even if you seem to almost never get much attention from men, if you follow the advice in this book, you will be on the fast track to finding the partner you desire and know deep down that you really deserve.

In this book we will talk about the essential qualities that all men will instantly look for in a woman. We will cover the initial attraction phase, right through to getting a man to fall completely in love with you! But we aren't going to stop there. We will go on to cover keeping a man's interest for the long haul and making sure he only has eyes for you even as more and more time passes by.

I will expose the truth about how much looks really matter to men and why, along with the features that men find most attractive in a woman. We will take a look at how we can seem far more approachable to the men that we find attractive, so that more of the men that you are interested in will feel like they can actually make the first move and strike up conversations with you.

This will cause more attractive men to make the first move with you and put in more effort to win you over. It will make them want to impress you and work for your affection. This will lead to them seeing you as a challenge and ultimately cause them to want a relationship even if that wasn't their original intent.

This will not just help you get and keep one man, but it will actually give you the choice of a selection men that will be willing to compete for your attention! This information will really put you in the driver's seat and let you determine what happens without any of the sitting around, waiting and wondering if he is going to text you back.

HOW MUCH DO LOOKS MATTER?

This is a topic of much controversy. Some people will tell you that looks don't matter at all, or at least that they shouldn't matter if someone is a decent enough person to look past the physical and judge you on your personality. These people will say that anyone who goes by looks are obviously a shallow person and you shouldn't be with someone like that anyway.

Other people will tell you that looks are extremely important and that it's the best way to attract the best caliber men to you. But what is the truth?

Men Are Visual

The first thing I feel that I need to mention on this topic is that men are very visual people. Far more visual than women in fact. As women, although we definitely notice a guy's looks, we tend to focus on personality a lot more as we are generally much more in tune with our emotional side. Men on the other hand focus far more on what their eyes are telling them.

This is just simple, basic psychology. This is why you could be having a stimulating conversation with a man but he may still be focusing on your boobs! A lot of women will take this as a sign of the man being a shallow person or sleazy. Well the fact is that it's built into men's psychology to run their eyes over a woman and 'check them out'. So you can't really blame them most of the time.

Of course if they are doing it in an obvious and creepy/suggestive way then they are definitely being sleazy, but if a guy is trying to talk to you but you catch him looking at your boobs or your bum then, if anything, that a good sign as it means he's interested and finds you attractive.

Does Weight Matter?

It's built into our biology to look for mates that are physically fit and in good shape. It's not just simply because women with better figures look better, because what defines what we find attractive has been ingrained into us by evolution.

What we just take for granted as being considered attractive these days is actually a remnant from our evolution. Our ancestors brains would tell them to automatically look for a physically fit mate to breed with, simply because by breeding with a strong mate in good physical shape would result in the best and strongest offspring and is therefore best for the future of the species.

So when men look at physically fit women and find them attractive, it's not just because they think it looks nicer, it's because their brain is programmed to look for that physique in a mate. So is it really any surprise that men prefer more slender women as appose to women who are overweight and out of shape? Of course not. Men are just doing what comes naturally when they have a preference for fit, healthy women.

Now, I'm not saying you need to be thin, you just need to be healthy. In my experience, most men don't really find stick thin women that attractive anyway. They tend to like women who are in shape and look healthy.

Men also love the curves of a woman's body. This is another thing that their brains are telling them to look for without probably even consciously realizing it. They find curves attractive because their brains associate it with sex and reproduction, also as a result of our evolution. So generally most men would find a woman with all the curves in the right places far more attractive than a skinny woman.

So to be at your optimal level of attractiveness with regards to your body weight, you just need to be healthy. This will usually require eating right and having an active lifestyle, that's all.

Being too skinny is as detrimental to your chances with men as being overweight. This is because both are seen by our brains as being unhealthy and therefore unattractive. So, if you want to attract men, you really do need to get your body weight in check if you haven't already.

You by no means have to be 'perfect' because that simply doesn't exist. By just by maintaining a healthy body weight, eating well and keeping active, you will increase your chance of attracting men to you 100 fold.

Personal Hygiene

Having good personal hygiene and taking care of your appearance is of vital importance when trying to attract men. You may think of men as people who perhaps wouldn't notice these things as much because they generally aren't quite as clean and well-groomed as women, but that doesn't mean they don't look for it in a partner. Slightly hypocritical I know, but women are seen as being the 'fairer sex' after all, so you're going to have to put some effort in.

Especially now in the modern era, there are a lot of men who take care of themselves a lot more and pay much more attention to male grooming. This can be seen by the massive boom in the male grooming and male toiletries industry. 20 years ago this industry wasn't exactly booming but today it's worth over an estimated 20 billion dollars a year and growing fast!

So it's more important than ever for us women to look after our personal hygiene as more and more men will be paying attention to it. I can tell you from experience that my male friends have stopped seeing women on a couple of occasions that I can think of, purely because of their breath! One even said that everything else about this woman was great and they were attractive (I saw a photo and she was very attractive indeed) but just because her breath was bad, he couldn't stand to kiss her and stopped seeing her because of it!

So you really don't want to be putting off guys over silly things like that which are easily remedied, especially if they like everything else about you. All it takes is a shower a day, clean clothes, deodorant, brushing your teeth regularly and a bit of mouthwash! It's not too much to ask right?

PERSONALITY

Many of the personality traits that men look for in a partner are fairly obvious, but some may be slightly more surprising. To find out which ones matter a lot and which ones are deal breakers or deal makers, we have to look a bit deeper into male psychology.

Nagging

Guys absolutely hate it when women nag them and are persistent when asking them to do something that they really don't want to. There are two parts to why men really hate nagging so much. It's not simply because it's annoying, which it obviously is. There are more deep rooted psychological issues as to why nagging is such a deal breaker for men.

The first point I need to make on this subject is that men like to feel like they are a leader and the man of the house. They like to be strong and make decisions. If you are nagging him and telling him to do things, this undermines his manhood and makes him feel week.

Making a man feel this way when he is around you is one of the fastest ways to not only put him off you but also put yourself off of him. When you perceive him as being less of a man and less of a leader you will quickly loose respect for him.

The second reason why men hate nagging so much is because they like to feel independent. By nagging him, you will effectively be smothering him and taking away some of that all-important independence. If you make him feel this way, like he is backed into a corner with consistent nagging then, if it continues, don't be surprised if he walks.

Sensitivity

This may be a surprising one but men are actually quite often more sensitive and, in some cases, more emotional than women. This may sound crazy to some people but it's completely true. Men have plenty of emotion going on, they just tend to try not to show it as much as women because they feel as if they are expected to look strong and unemotional.

Men may seem unemotional and cold at times, but they aren't. They are just holding it in because they are uncomfortable with looking weak and showing that they are upset. They have been told their whole life that men are strong and don't talk about these things, so you can't blame them for doing this. But there will come a point where they really open up to you, this is make or break so be ready for it.

Most men don't like to admit, talk about and show their emotions as much, so when they do show them, you know that it's important. In which case you have to be very understanding and show them sensitivity. Men love this and if you give them this, seeing as they don't like showing this side of themselves to just anyone, you will be that one person that they can really open up to. This will cause them to form an incredibly strong bond with you on an emotional level that they don't have with anyone else.

This one is so important. I know a lot of women won't even try to understand their man's feelings and emotions and then complain that he doesn't talk to them enough. This is a super-fast relationship killer. If you want your man to be open with you and talk to you about how he is feeling, then you need to be extremely understanding and emotionally supportive. If you do this, he will be yours for the long haul.

Conflict Resolution

Men love a woman who is calm, good at resolving arguments in a rational way and non-argumentative. Unfortunately, even I will admit that this isn't a strong point of many women at all. As women, although some of us may not admit it, most of us thrive on emotion and arguments stir up a whole lot of emotions. There are a lot of women out there who love a good shouting match with their partner as it allows them to let out built up aggression and essentially use their man as a verbal punching bag for all of their built up stress and tension. This is not healthy. At all.

Woman who do this will drive men away faster than if they were jabbing them with a cattle prod. Maybe a slight exaggeration but you get the point. Men hate arguing, so being argumentative and someone who doesn't try to resolve conflict quickly and easily is a huge deal breaker for pretty much every man on the planet.

If you have argued a lot with previous partners and ended up shouting a lot, then you will need to work on your conflict resolution or risk losing more perfectly good partners in the years to come. You really can't expect a men to stay with you if you're constantly arguing and shouting at him.

If you need to let out tension and shout then you can have a good moan, but direct your anger elsewhere. You can tell him about what you're annoyed about at work in an aggressive, angry way and let out some tension that way. As long as you aren't screaming at him and causing him to argue back, then this won't cause him nearly as much stress.

Invite Him In

Men love it when women don't revolve their life around them, but instead you invite them into your personal world and make them a huge part of your life. So invite him to meet your friends and family. Invite him to do things that you like to do an involve him in your life.

This will open him up to a whole new range of people, places and activities that he would have never done without you in his life. Anyone, both men and women love it when their partners do this.

You obviously have to take part in his life too and have your personal life that's just between you two, but also invite him into your world. He will feel far more connected with you if you do this and he will find aspects of this that he loves and that he won't want to lose. It could be something as simple as your mothers roast dinners or he might fall in love with your friends dog! It could be lots of things like this and you will feel great having someone else to share your life with.

This also helps with your friends. You have probably experienced this if you have a long term relationship. When you start spending more and more time with your new partner, your friends may become unhappy that you don't have as much time for them. By involving him in your life and doing things with him and your friends at the same time, you will keep everyone happy. He will get to be involved in your word and your friends will get to still see you often.

Obviously everyone needs time away from their partner and to just be able to see their friends on their own, so allow time for that too, but try to involve him often.

Compromise

A woman who compromises on decisions is incredibly appealing to a man. If you are too stubborn and set in your ways on things, he will feel like you are wearing the trousers and become frustrated very quickly.

You need to let your man be a man and make decisions. If you keep making all the decisions on where you are going to go and what you're going to do or eat, then he will feel like he is just being pushed around. That's no way for a man to act, so you need to compromise on what you would ideally want to do sometimes in order to let him be a man and take control once in a while.

For a guy, the importance of this cannot be overstated. The whole dynamic of the relationship revolves around this and the joint decision making process. Also, if you do go along with what he wants to do and you do compromise, letting him make the decisions and feel like a man, don't make it clear that you aren't happy about it. Making him feel bad about putting you out is just as bad as flat out telling him he can't make the decision in the first place.

This is a cruel mind game that a lot of women (and men) play. They will tell you that you can do whatever you want, but then when you do it, they make you feel bad about it. This is another relationship killer and it's so obvious what you're doing, it's not sneaky or clever at all, so avoid it! If you go along with something, even if it's not what you would ideally be doing, try to make the best of it and don't make him feel bad about it.

So a good example of this would be when you're deciding what to have for dinner or where to go to eat, you can tell him to decide and tell him that wherever he wants to go is fine with you. Then, even though it's only a small decision, he will feel like he's being the man and making the decision. Doing this kind of thing once in a while is great for a balanced and healthy relationship.

This allows him the opportunity to try and make you happy. If he has made all the decisions and he see you happy as a result of those decisions, that is what will make him feel like a man.

Let Him Help You

Following on from the last point, as I think it's really important and something that not enough women realize, men love it when women show the man they are with how happy he makes them by what he's doing.

If he feels like you value him and that he is doing the right things to make you happy, it will make him feel like far more of a man. Feeling like a man isn't just about doing DIY or having a beer and watching the game. It's mostly about what they can do for their woman. So let him help you.

This is why DIY is such a big point for a man. I had an ex who wanted to fix the broken plug on my hair dryer a few years ago, but I didn't let him do it. I told him that I was going to let my dad do it at the weekend when he came down to visit me. He complained and said it was just some simple wiring that he had done before and that he could do it in 2 minutes. I still didn't let him fix it for me, just because I trusted my dad to do it more than I trusted him to. This really bothered him and at the time I didn't really understand why.

I now see that this was basically telling him he wasn't enough of a man to help me and that I didn't trust him to give me help. This is a huge masculinity killer and I cringe a bit when I think back to it now. I should have let him help me and let him feel like a man. I'm sure he could have fixed it absolutely fine.

So let your man help you and when he does, show him how much you appreciate it. After all, he is helping you because he wants to feel like he can look after his woman like a real man should, so you should appreciate that he is doing that. Don't just show him your appreciation with your words either, you can show it with your touch, your smile and the way you act when he is making an effort to help you. Doing this regularly will make him feel on top of the world and like he is making a real difference to your life.

STAND OUT FROM THE CROWD

When you're trying to either catch a man's attention or keep it for the long haul, you need to stand out. If you're going for a man who is a bit of a catch, you have to be realistic and consider the possibility that he has other options available to him.

To combat this, I have some fantastic, simple tips to really make you stand out and catch his attention more than the other women that he could potentially be interested in.

Thank Him

This one really is simple, just remember to thank him for the things he does for you and tell him how much you appreciate it. If you're letting him know that you appreciate the effort he is putting in, he will feel like a million dollars.

While the other women are expecting him to pay for meals and expecting him to open the car door for them, when he does these things for you, tell him that you appreciate it. You can tell him how sweet he is and how much of a gentleman he is and just generally show him with your body language and the way you act how happy his efforts make you.

This will really make you stand out in his mind as someone genuine who really makes him feel like the effort he is putting in is worth it. Most other women will seem like stuck up cows compared to you if you start doing this!

Any man who is considering having a relationship with you will think that he can make you happy. But when he gets that confirmation and feedback from you that he is actively making you happy, he will realize that he is achieving it and this will not only make him feel like you're far more special than the other women who didn't appreciate him but it will make him try even harder to keep making you happy.

When he gets this feedback about how great he is right now, he will take that information and implant it into his self-image. If he thinks you are viewing him as a great guy, he will start to believe it. Self-image is such a powerful thing, it dictates almost all of our daily interactions, so if you make him feel like a 'super boyfriend' then that's what he will believe and become. It puts him in the mindset of someone who makes their partner incredibly happy and he will want to keep doing it.

To further enforce this, people like living up to expectations, so if he feels like you view him in this way he will actively try to live up to your expectations of him. This doesn't work if you flat out tell men what you expect of them, you need to make them feel that you have high expectations based on how great they are and how amazing they have made you feel. So you want them to think that they are the ones who have set their own high standards by being great, not just because you have high standards personally.

Positive Energy

Okay so that heading may sound a bit 'hippy' but let me explain how powerful giving off positive energy really is. So let me set the scene. There is a girl who obviously spends every day in the gym, she's walking down the street in hot pants and a bikini top, she's looking great and showing off a lot of skin. You're standing there talking to a guy and his attention wanders and he starts checking her out. You can tell he would prefer to be talking to her.

Most women would think the best way to combat this is to lose weight and try and look as good as that other girl and get a body like hers. Wrong. The best way to combat the competition is to give off positive energy and good vibes. If you're talking to a guy and you're showing a real zest for life and letting your happiness shine through, he won't be able to ignore it.

There may be other women around who are attractive, but if you have a great positive energy surround you and he can feel it, he will be drawn into you. So smile and show your happiness and positivity in your body language, your facial expressions and the way you talk. If you do this, the girl walking the other side of the street with the bad case of 'resting bitch face' won't stand a chance!

MIND GAMES

Like it or not, mind games are a part of dating and relationships. Everyone plays mind games to some extent. I'm not saying that mind games are a good thing and that you shouldn't be honest and transparent with your partner or the guy that you want to be with, but by using a few simple techniques that will appeal to male psychology, you can get him chasing after you in no time!

These little tricks that you can use could be the difference between having the men you want actively chasing after you and having them be uninterested and leaving you to do all of the work.

Playing it Cool

In the beginning, when you're first getting to know a guy, it's very important to play it cool and not come on too strongly. If you make it clear that you're extremely interested right away then you run the risk of two things happening.

Number one is that you could scare him off. It's a well-known fact that some men are allergic to any form of commitment. Given time, these men may well slip gradually into a relationship without getting freaked out as the natural progression of your relationship takes place. But if you scare them off by being too needy at first, you may lose someone who could have turned into a long term relationship.

The second thing you will do by coming on too strong is you will take away the challenge and the thrill of the chase. Men like to see women as being hard to get, it makes them feel like they are achieving something rather than just taking something that has just fallen on their lap. By making them work for your attention, even if they don't truly need to as they have it already, they will appreciate you far more when they finally get you.

If you take away the challenge not only will they feel like they can mess you about, cancel plans they have with you without having to worry and only text you when they feel like it, but they may also start to think there must be a reason why you're so keen. This may lead them to think that you're not good enough for them seeing as you're so interested. Or they may also think that you must be desperate and not have any other options.

By playing it cool you will keep them thinking about you more often and trying to win your attention. They may also even see you as being out of their league just because they are having to work hard to get you.

In order to play it cool, you don't have to ignore, not reply to their messages or put them down in any way. Doing this will actually put them off! You just need a nice balance. You can show your interest in more subtle ways and not give too much away too quickly. Just keep them guessing every step of the way and drop hints that you're interested without being obvious about it.

Feel free to flirt a bit while playing it cool. Just playful flirting, nothing too serious or suggestive. The key is just not showing too much interest but giving them enough to keep them interested themselves. So don't get carried away, especially with flirting. Don't be overly sexual, teasing and putting subtle ideas in their head is much more effective than going over the top.

So, show a bit of interest to keep their attention and keep them working on getting more out of you, but don't give too much away. That is the essence of playing it cool and it works wonders!

Limiting Your Time Together

I have seen far too many relationships end before they have properly started simply because people get too carried away and spend 5 or 6 days a week together just after they have met.

My dad is the worst for doing this. As soon as he meets a woman he starts to see her pretty much every day and, perhaps unsurprisingly, every relationship he has had since separating from my mother has fizzled out far too quickly.

If you see too much of someone right off the bat you run a very high risk of them getting sick of you and taking your company for granted. Even the most tolerant people will get bored of someone's company if they spend every day with them. Obviously further down the line, once you have gotten used to each other, you can step things up and get more serious. For the first few months at least you want to limit your time with them.

Seeing each other too much will also cause more tension and arguments which you definitely want to avoid in the early stages. If you kick things off with arguing once or twice a week simply because you're getting far too comfortable too quickly, you will set off serious warning bells in each other's heads.

The other thing you will do by limiting the time you spend with them is make them realize that you have a life! If you just suddenly start seeing them almost every day, they will think that you maybe don't have many friends or that you're a bit of a loner. Obviously nobody want to think that you are only seeing them because you have nothing better to do.

Perhaps the main and most important thing that seeing them less than you may like will do, is make them want to see you even more. If you see them too much they will take it for granted. If you leave them wanting more every time you leave them however, they will appreciate the time they do spend with you far more. This will make them far more attentive, interested and more caring during the time that you do spend together. Quality over quantity definitely applies here!

THE IMPORTANCE OF SEX

You may or may not have seen this one coming! Amazing sex and being sexually compatible with your partner is vital to the longevity of any relationship. Sex is much more than what Cosmo makes it out to be. There's not just simple little techniques that you should use, there's whole new levels of intimacy and new levels of connection you can find with your partner through really fulfilling sex. This applies to men just as much as it does to women.

But having a great, satisfying sex life is not the only way sex can be used to improve your success in relationships. You can also use a lack of sex in a very clever way in the early stages to get guys who may normally just be after a sex buddy to convert into a dedicated and loyal long term boyfriend!

Sex and Dating

So let's start by talking about what I just mentioned. Sex is so useful when dating, because you can withhold it! There are a lot of guys out there who will just date women and act like they are serious about them in order to get women to sleep with them. It happens a lot.

So what can we do about all too common this problem? Well, just don't have sex until you have got them into a relationship that they are willing to admit to publicly! Once they are willing to introduce you to their friends and publicly tell people that you are their girlfriend, you can be pretty sure they are serious about you.

If however, you have only gone on three dates together and you sleep with them, it's easy for them to have not fallen for you yet and to just walk away, no matter how much of a connection you may have felt with them.

Even guys who were just dating you because they found you attractive and want to sleep with you will easily start to grow attached. This is because guys don't like to fail when it comes to women. So they will keep trying even harder if you don't put out.

Men can't stand it when women are interested but aren't ready to sleep with them yet. It drives them crazy, in a good way! It will make them work much harder and while they are doing so, they will grow far more attached to you during the process.

There are some men who may just think it's not worth the effort just to get you into bed, but those are the guys you want to avoid anyway, no matter how much you may like them back. But in my experience, for the most part, this will convert guys who originally just wanted to sleep with you, into dedicated boyfriends. I have seen this happen with my friends and it's worked for me.

They even joke about it afterwards saying things like, "Yeah she got her claws into me and I couldn't get away!" Where as if they had just slept with them, they would have not had the chance to 'get their claws into them' because they would have lost interest.

The other side effect of this is that the men you are dating will respect you so much more for having the self-respect and self-control to not just succumb to your desires and sleep with someone that you had only been on a few dates with. This causes men to really see you as being different from the other women they may have dated in the past and want to take things further with you.

Having Great Sex to Keep a Man Coming Back

Most women have had the problem of having sex with a man or having sex with him a few times and them he suddenly loses interest. Well, the harsh truth is, if you're giving him incredible sex, he would most likely be coming back for more. If you're having average, standard sex then there is a chance he will lose interest or move on to someone else if he's not overly interested in your personality and company just yet.

Or maybe you're in a long term relationship and your man is losing interest in having sex and you're worried about him either leaving you or trying to find what he missing out on with you elsewhere?

Well, for the rest of this chapter I'm going to talk about how you can have truly mind blowing sex and how you can be in the top percentage of women who really know how to satisfy a man in the bedroom.

Truly fantastic sex is very rare these days. When you first start a sexual relationship with someone, any sex is great sex because it's new and exciting and you get to do all of these things with them for the first time. But the sad reality is that, as with all things, if you do it enough then it will get boring sooner or later.

Sexual Energy

Sex doesn't start with foreplay like some people may imagine. Sex actually starts on an invisible and energetic level before you even touch your partner. The anticipation and lead up to sex is often more exciting and mentally stimulating than the act itself.

That excitement is so important to your sex life. If you can arouse your partner in a situation where he can't act upon it, it will add to the anticipation drastically. For example, say you're having a meal around a friend's house and there are other people around, you could send him a sneaky text saying something sexual that you would not normally say. This will not only surprise him which will get him excited, but it will also cause a buildup of sexual energy between you during the time when you can't act upon it or even talk about it. Then when he finally gets you home, all of that built up energy and mental stimulation will result in some really great sex!

Although the energy doesn't have to be so blatantly sexual. Having a great vibe and energy between you in general will hugely increase the intimacy between you and your partner. Just by paying more attention to them in general will dramatically affect your sex life.

The Importance of Kissing

Kissing is a massively underrated part of sex. Most people focus on direct sexual pleasure and just dive pretty much straight into it, only seeing kissing as necessary step to bridge the gap between lying in bed and reaching below their partners clothes to get to the good part!

Deep sensual kissing with your tongue is often forgotten about, but it can really heighten the mood and stimulate both parties. Kissing is often seen as not being a big deal but that's because people don't tend to focus on it and they just see it as a means to an end in almost all circumstances.

Try really focusing on your kissing and try kissing deeper and harder than you usually would do. Just this tiny difference in how you're kissing them will cause your partner to quickly realize this isn't just normal sex that they are about to receive!

Compliment Their Body

Complimenting your partners body is a great way to get them to give you more effort than they usually would do. This will not only boost their confidence which will make them want to live up to your words but it will also help them feel more comfortable with you which is vital to a good sex life.

This may seem strange with long term partners as you will probably be quite used to their body by now so there won't be many surprises, but you can comment on a change even if there isn't one. Or you could even do it in a light hearted way if you find it awkward. For example a funny line like, "Has this thing grown?" will boost your partners confidence to no end!

You should also compliment them on their technique too, but be careful with this one! Only compliment them on things you honestly do like otherwise they may keep doing something that doesn't really do much for you just because you complimented them on it once.

Slow Things Down

Taking things slow and having slow rhythmic sex can really heighten sensation and feels as good for men as it does for women. Slow sex is far more intimate so it's great to throw in from time to time.

It should give both of you the time to really focus on the feeling and sensations. This also helps men to last longer and so improves female satisfaction. Obviously you can finish off faster but just start off slow and see the difference it makes.

The longer it takes both you are your partner to climax then the better it will be when it does eventually happen. People now use a technique that makes the most of this fact, which you may have already heard of, called edging. It's a funny name but it does actually work. You basically get to the point of orgasm but then stop just before and go really slow again for a while and let the feeling subside. If you repeat this a few times, when you finally do climax it will be much more intense.

So get your partner to tell you when he is getting close and then stop, before slowly easing into it again. This will drive him crazy and it will make sex last longer for you, which is obviously something that most of us ladies will love!

Be Vocal

Some of you may already have this one covered! However, some women are much more quiet and less vocal in the bedroom. Now, I'm not talking about dirty talk, although some guys really do love hearing their woman coming out with some really dirty words, I'm talking about groaning to show your pleasure.

Men absolutely love getting feedback in the form of moans and groans as they are having sex. They will see it as a sign that they are doing well and this will fill them with confidence and spur them on to try even harder and put in even more effort.

Also the sound of a woman moaning in their ear and expressing their sexual pleasure is a huge turn on for guys, so don't hold back!

CONCLUSION

So, as you can probably tell, if you follow this guide you will remove all of the major stumbling blocks that end up getting in the way of a successful relationship. That's what it's about really. We aren't trying to trick guys into falling in love with us, we're just making sure that the process of attracting and keeping a guy goes as smoothly as possible. If you follow the tips in this book then that's exactly what will happen.

Now, one thing that you need to remember is that you can do all of these things and make yourself as easy to date as possible, but if you're not out there meeting guys then nothing is going to happen for you.

The simplest way to meet new men is to head out to social events or go and try out some new fun activities where there are guys around. Then when you see a guy you like, throw a look his way and maybe a cheeky smile. This is all it takes for most guys to approach you if they are physically attracted to you. You may need to make eye contact a few times or go stand or sit on your own for a minute before he has the confidence to come up to you, but it will work.

Then from that point, just follow the advice I have given you in this book and you will be on the fast track to success with men.

FINAL THOUGHTS

Well I think that about covers it! Thank you so much for reading this book, I really appreciate it!

If you would also consider taking the time to leave me an honest review on this book on Amazon I would be extremely appreciative of your feedback.

You can find links to all of my previous books full of great advice for women by simply searching for "Amelia Farris" on Amazon. Thanks again for reading and I hopefully speak to you all in the next book!

Made in the USA
San Bernardino, CA
11 September 2018